THEOLOGICAL
EXISTENCE TO-DAY!

(A Plea for Theological Freedom)

by
KARL BARTH

Translated by R. BIRCH HOYLE

D1730442

WIPF & STOCK · Eugene, Oregon

Wipf and Stock Publishers
199 W 8th Ave, Suite 3
Eugene, OR 97401

Theological Existence To-Day!
A Plea for Theological Freedom
By Barth, Karl and Hoyle, R. Birch
Copyright©1933 Theologischer Verlag Zurich
ISBN 13: 978-1-61097-572-8
Publication date 5/24/2011
Previously published by Hodder & Stoughton, 1933

© of the German original version
Theologischer Verlag Zürich

FOREWORD

THE chief motive we have for preparing this translation for the benefit of English readers is our deep sense of the importance of Dr. Barth's brochure for all sections of Christendom. This message is a solemn call to all the Churches to reflect upon the necessity for allowing the sovereign rule of God's Word in all the affairs of the Christian Church.

There is no desire on our part to deepen any antagonism towards the German people. Dr. Barth deals with measures, not men : with principles and not politics or persons. His analysis of the various mental attitudes now existing within the Churches of Germany is of first-rate importance and value to those who desire to understand the real facts of the situation, theologically and ecclesiastically. First principles are sought for and found by this penetrating mind. The great principles of liberty of conscience, of freedom for theological thought and pulpit ministrations, the limits set to secular authorities as regards the autonomy of the Christian Church, the Bible view and hope for devout souls in turbulent times, the proper function of the Christian ministry towards peoples and nations, are here discussed in the spirit of awe and reverence by one who " trembles at the Word of God."

A few words may be necessary to explain some features of this translation. The cross-headings do not occur in the German text : they are inserted to guide the reader, and indicate the gist of the thought in each section. In the German text there is a copious use of italicised words : these have been reproduced in order to show where Dr. Barth would have the emphasis to be placed. The lengthy sentences of the German text have been broken up into shorter sentences in accord with English idiom. But it is hoped that nothing of importance has been omitted owing to this. As far as possible the attempt has been made to capture some of the thunder roll and tone, which make it no easy task to make Barth's style such a massive force in another tongue than his own. A few notes have been added in order to make somewhat clearer references which will be perfectly plain to those who have followed the course of events in Germany of late. We think this small book is a document of historic importance for understanding the Church situation in Germany to-day.

May we, as members of different sections of the One Christian Church—one is a Baptist, the other a Quaker—express our thankfulness to God for sending to our generation so mighty a prophet ?

(*Signed*) R. BIRCH HOYLE

CARL HEATH

THEOLOGICAL EXISTENCE TO-DAY!

FOR a good while back I have been frequently asked if I had nothing to say about the concerns and problems affecting the German Church nowadays. I can no longer ignore these requests, coming as they do from many of my former pupils and others who share my theological outlook. But I must at once make clear that the essence of what I attempt to contribute to-day bearing upon these anxieties and problems cannot be made the theme of a particular manifesto, for the simple reason that at Bonn here, with my students in lectures and courses, I endeavour to carry on theology, and only theology, now as previously, and as if nothing had happened. Perhaps there is a slightly increased tone, but without direct allusions : something like the chanting of the hours by the Benedictines near by in the *Maria Laach*, which goes on undoubtedly without break or interruption, pursuing the even tenor of its way even in the Third *Reich*. I regard the pursuit of theology as the proper attitude to adopt : at any

rate it is one befitting Church-politics, and, indi-
rectly, even politics. And I expect that this
communication, without " particular messages," will
be heard and interpreted by the students committed to my charge, as well as may be, amidst the
stirring happenings of our time.

In the matter of speaking and having an audience
I have ample reasons for being content to keep
within the limits of my vocation as a theological
professor. I did not pass beyond these bounds
when I accepted an invitation to collaborate with
other members of the Reformed Church persuasion
when recently issuing two theological manifestos.
The part I took in this affair has been rightly interpreted, and I think those manifestos received the
finest compliment, for they were blamed as lacking.
It was said that they did not face actualities and
the facts of life, they did not tackle the problems
of the day. If, dear friends at home and abroad,
I have now been persuaded to speak " to the
situation," as it is expected of me, it can only
be in the form of a question. The question is :
" Would it not be better if one did *not* speak ' to
the situation,' *but*, each one within the limits of
his vocation, if he spoke ' ad rem ' ? " In other
words, to consider and work out the presuppositions

needed every day for speaking " ad rem," as it is needed to-day*—not to-day for the first time—and yet it is needed to-day! A slight elucidation of this question can alone be my theme, if so be anyone wants to hear me on the stirrings now afoot.

WHAT THEOLOGICAL EXISTENCE PRESUPPOSES

The one thing that must not happen to us who are theological professors, is our abandoning our job through becoming zealous for some cause we think to be good. Our existence as theologians is our life within the Church, and, of course, as appointed preachers and teachers within the Church.

There are some things about which there is unanimity within the Church. One is, that there is no more urgent demand in the whole world than that which the Word of God makes, viz. that the Word be preached and heard. At all costs this

* Dr. Barth explains, in a separate note, what the events of " to-day," June 24th, 1933, were. 1. Councillor Jaeger was appointed " Church Commissioner " for the whole of Prussia. 2. Herr Hundt, of the Supreme Consistorial Court in Berlin, and General Superintendent Schian, in Breslau, were removed from their offices. 3. Dr. von Bodelschwingh, the Provisional *Reichs*-Bishop was forced to retire. 4. The Central Church Press Bureau in Berlin was put under " German Christian " control. 5. The Prussian Delegation to the Church Conference at Eisenach was deprived of its authority.

demand has to be discharged by the world and the Church itself, cost what it may. Another thing there is agreement about is, that the Word of God clears out of the way everything that might oppose, so that it *will* triumph over us and all other opponents, for the reason that it *has* triumphed already, once for all, over us and on our behalf, and over all its other opponents. For the Word, " was crucified, dead, buried, raised again the third day, sitteth at the right hand of the Father." Within the Church it is agreed that God " upholds *all* things by the Word of His power " (*Hebrews* i. 3) : that He supplies answer to *every* question, that He allows righteousness to experience *all* anxieties, that He sustains all that He has made, and leads it to its truest end, that *no* thing can subsist and flourish without His Word. Again, within the Church it is agreed that it is good for man to depend upon the Word of God, and that this is his only good in time and eternity, to rely upon it with all his heart, all his mind, soul and all his powers. Further, it is the unanimous opinion within the Church, that God is never for us in the world, that is to say, in our space and time, except in this His Word, and that this Word for us has no other name and content but Jesus Christ, and that Jesus

Christ is never to be found on our behalf save each day afresh in the Holy Scriptures of the Old and New Testaments. One is not in the Church at all if he is not of a mind with the Church in these things.

And, particularly as preachers and teachers of the Church, we are at one in fear but also in joy, that we are called to serve the Word of God within the Church and in the world by our preaching and our teaching. We agree, too, that with the fulfilment of our calling we not only see ourselves stand or fall, but we see everything that is important to us in this world, however precious or great it be, standing or falling. So that to us no concern can be more pressing, no hope more moving than the concern and hope of our ministry. No friend can be dearer than one who helps us in this ministry, no foe more hateful than he that wants to hinder us in this ministry.

We are agreed about this too, that alongside of this first business, as the meaning of our labour and our rest, our diligence and relaxation, our love and our scorn, we brook no second as a rival. But we regard every second or third thing that may and should incite us as included and taken up in this first concern, and condemned or blessed

13   B

thereby. On these things we agree or we are not preachers and teachers of the Church. And this is what is meant by what we term our " Theological existence," viz. that in the midst of our life in other aspects, as, say, men, fathers and sons, as Germans, as citizens, thinkers, as having hearts ever in unrest, etc., the Word of God may be what it simply is, and only can be to us, and taxes our powers, particularly as preachers and teachers, to the full as the Word alone can and must do.

THE MINISTER'S TEMPTATION TO-DAY

To-day we can lose our existence as theologians and teachers, which consists in our attachment to God's Word and plying our calling particularly to the ministry of the Word. To put it in other words, to-day, more than ever, we can neglect to affirm our life's calling. Or, better expressed still, it is possible for us to find that our theological life will no longer be allowed to us, as it ought to be granted us anew every day, just because we forget to pray and reach out for it, and now to-day, more than ever, we should do our part so that it may be given to us. For the mighty temptation of this age, which appears in every shape possible, is that we no longer appreciate the intensity and exclusiveness of the demand which the Divine Word makes as such when looking at the force of other demands: so that in our anxiety in face of existing dangers we no longer put our whole trust in the authority of God's Word, but we think we ought to come to its aid with all sorts of contrivances, and we thus throw quite aside our confidence in the Word's power to triumph. That is to say, we think ourselves capable of facing, solving and moulding definite problems better from some other source than that from and by means of God's Word. By doing this we show that we do not esteem God to be a working factor in anything as Creator, Reconciler, and Redeemer. That our hearts are thus divided between God's Word and all other sorts of things which, avowedly or tacitly, we invest with Divine glory. By so doing we demonstrate that our hearts are not in contact with God's Word. And this means that under the stormy assault of " principalities, powers, and rulers of this world's darkness," we seek for God elsewhere than in His Word, and seek His Word somewhere else than in Jesus Christ, and seek Jesus Christ elsewhere than in the Holy Scriptures of the Old and New Testaments. And so we become as those who do not seek for God at all

And all this, though the very opposite is what is agreed upon within the Church !

How, then, ought we to be in the Church ? The special form of this temptation to us, the Church's preachers and teachers is, that possibly and actually there can be something like rivalry between our vocation within the Church and this or that other calling which is different : in such a way that we feel driven and forced to let this or that different calling be played off against or parallel with our Church vocation, or let that other interpret and shape our proper Church vocation. That we see ourselves and the men to whom we are appointed standing and falling under utterly different conditions from the condition that rightly directs our ministry. So that the secondary or the third thing, which we well know ought to be absorbed in the first concern, as an operative factor, comes to be first, coincides with it, and finally steps into the place of the first. And thereby, the really first concern, and our particular vocation, become hopelessly lost. Although we, as preachers and teachers within the Church, in a quite different sense were in accord ! We are then no longer preachers and teachers of the Church ; we are politicians, and Church politicians at that ! It is no disgrace to be a politician or even a Church politician ; it holds a special esteem : but it is something else to be a theologian. It can always denote damage to the theologian's existence as such, when he becomes a politician or a Church politician. To-day this seems to be pre-eminently the case. And therefore it is time to say, that under no circumstances should we, as theologians, forsake our theological existence and exchange our rights as " first-born " for " a mess of pottage." Or, said positively, that now, one and all, within the Church as she has borne us by means of the Word, and within the incomparable sphere of our vocation we must *abide*, or (if we have left it) *turn back* into the Church and into the sphere of our vocation, at all costs, by putting all regards and concerns behind.

THE PROBLEMS DISCUSSED

While I am writing this on the eve of June 25th, 1933, I will try to illustrate what I mean by taking as examples three of the problems that occupy us to-day. It happens quite fortunately that these problems, severally and collectively, deal pre-eminently with the decisions reached to-day, viz.

17

the establishment of a State-Commissioner for the Church, and his first orders, have entered upon a quite different stage. My remarks may not be actually " to the situation," i.e. the attendant circumstances, but " to the business," *ad rem.* I may perhaps be better understood according to the problem by which I illustrate my thesis. The problem, certainly, has not been solved by those decisions which, however, in its form hitherto has, so to speak, become an historical problem.

I—THE CRIES FOR CHURCH REFORM

When the political movement of this year had already passed beyond the first decisive steps of its triumph, there was taken up from different quarters at once, the cry that the German Evangelical Church must now proceed to a far-reaching new-ordering of its external relationships. Corresponding advances have been made which were accompanied by a varied taking part by theologians and Church members in speeches and counter-speeches. The initiative and leading in this new ordering, judging from what has happened to-day, was taken out of the Church's control. In order to discuss and analyse the situation now arisen, it is necessary to raise the question : " How did those *outcries for reform of the Church* comport with legitimacy, particularly at that time ? "

This statement may be ventured, that even a *reform* of the Church, chiefly affecting its external aspect, ought to spring from the internal requirement of the Church's life itself : it ought to issue from obedience to the Word of God, or else it is no reform of the *Church.* In any case, we shall have to admit, that all of us who have any share in the life of the Church, were well aware of the most serious need for improving so many Church relationships, and aware too, of the projects in the air everywhere from of old and from recent times. But still, at the commencement of this remarkable year we had no inkling of such an acute necessity for proceeding to action. That is to say, on the one hand, aware of the existence of problems and requirements of Church life which had been so burning, and on the other hand, aware of the existence on the spot of the deep insights, and of the great forces, which would seem to have made this undertaking now to be our own responsibility, and one full of hope. At that time, at any rate, we did not think of or know of any command to act in this way issuing as God's

Word to us. If a change has come over what existed in the early part of the year, and since, how did it happen ?

The proceedings since then, as regards the so-called Church of the *Reich* and what is connected therewith, have neither been settled speedily, nor been carried through with purpose, decision and unanimity, nor (as this has been glaringly illustrated by the event of to-day, June 24th) has it been very successful. If, on account of a burning necessity, and consequently with adequate force, a Reform of the Church had been undertaken, a Reform under the constraint of the Word of God, then would it not have worn a different look, in its development during the past few months ? I might attribute this defect to the fact that it was not so : not at all due to the personalities of the Churchmen who took part therein ! But let it also not be said too hurriedly, that in the Evangelical Church, as a " Church under the Cross," that it is impossible for it to be otherwise than obviously human, all-too-human, even in its palmiest ages, and that, in consequence, the manifest weakness of what has been done up till now, may be regarded, so to speak, as a normal phenomenon. The real Church under the Cross is the Church of the Holy Ghost whose activities must

still in themselves, amid all the feebleness and foolish-
ness of men, possess something profoundly gladden-
ing and peaceful, something Sabbatical, reverential.
An invisible yet subduing light never really
altogether departs from the spiritual decisions of
the Church—the light of a good conscience and
the promise of the forgiveness of sins amid the
weakness of the flesh. This light has not been
perceptible at all in the proceedings so far of Church
Reform. Nobody could have derived any satis-
faction, even in a moderate degree, from what has
been done at Loccum and Berlin. But this affirmation points to the fact that then, in spring, if reform
had been thought to be necessarily called for, it has
not taken place entirely in a legal manner with the
proper matters.

DID THE CHURCHES DECIDE THIS REFORM?

If, however, the question be asked, to what extent
at the time the resolution was taken " to build
this tower," it could have happened, that things
were not done in quite an adequate manner, then
it seems to me that one comes up against a remarkable and dangerous lack of clarity, because one most

fundamental, at the critical place. I mean the lack of clearness as to the relation between the Revolution, now a political *fait accompli*, and what the Church thought it had to plan and do in view of this event. We ask, Did the decision for this purpose and action issue from the Church itself? Or, in other words, From the Word of God heard by the Church? *Or*, was it a suggestion not inwardly necessary, but one arising from political enthusiasm, or, perchance political scheming: a decision not essentially of an ecclesiastical character, though embraced within and by the Church? If the first question cannot be answered in the affirmative, plainly, and with a good conscience, then the dissatisfaction and discord of the previous proceeding can be no puzzle. Rather, the first question cannot be affirmed outright and with a good conscience.

When I look directly at the most important official and private proclamations, issued at that time of the resolution and after it, I am continually brought up against the very strange phenomenon of certain political preambles in which, with an insistency surprising in a Church business, with a more or less openness and explicitness, the writers feel called upon, first and foremost, to give their positive judgment for, and appreciation of, the Revolution which took place in March, and also of the State thus formed. As one example out of many I cite the Appeal of the so-called " Committee of Three "* of date April 28th, 1933 :—

> " A mighty National Movement has captured and exalted our German Nation. An all-embracing reorganisation of the State is taking place within the awakened German people. We give our hearty assent to this turning-point of history. God has given us this : to Him be the glory.

> " Bound unitedly in God's Word, we recognise in the great events of our day a new commission of our Lord to His Churches."

In accordance with this proclamation there was often heard—from the Church side, mark you —such cries as, " The New State *needs* the Churches," and " The Church is ready to ' co-operate ' with the New State " : (a very competent writer added, " with its mighty forces.") On the background of this Proclamation of the Funda-

* Translator's note. The " Committee of Three " was composed of the following : Dr. Kapler, President of the Central Board of the German Evangelical Churches ; Bishop Marahrens, of Hanover (Lutheran) ; and Pastor Hesse of Elberfeld, an able educationalist.

mental Article of the newly-to-be-constituted Church, written afresh or in terms very similar, were then placarded the various proclamations, demands, programmes, and even confessions of faith, which were the object these announcements had in view.

What is to be said of all this ? Above all, this :— that what has happened must not be set down to an irresistible pressure from outside, to which the Church had to subject herself in order to salvage what she could in the new situation. The new Government, by the mouth of the *Reichs*-Chancellor, Adolf Hitler, declared on March 23rd :—

> " The rights of the Churches will not be diminished, nor their position as regards the State be altered."

On the same occasion he spoke of " an honourable joint-life in common between State and Church," but no mention was made of any " Gleichschaltung " (" assimilation ") whether from within or from without, on the part of the Church on behalf of the State. On the basis of this declaration of Hitler's, which has even been called the *Magna Carta* of the new Church within the new State, the Church was not asked to found itself upon this Fundamental

Article. And, apart from isolated attacks and mistakes, the State, or the Government of the State till now (i.e., June 25th) has nothing to be blamed for in this respect. Here I may recall the very precise declaration of Dr. Rust, the Prussian Minister for Education, in the " Kreuzzeitung," No. 125, for May 7th, 1933 :—

"For Prussia at any rate there exists no ground for anxiety that the State will interfere in the Church's inner life. Not even with its little finger will the State poke into those corners of the Church which are solely within her province to settle."

To-day one cannot disregard to what extent the latest events indicate only a very peculiar interpretation of these utterances and declarations, or that their repeal has become necessary in the eyes of the Government. But at the time when these statements were being made they pointed to an opportunity supplied to the Church, in view of which perhaps she durst not make herself responsible for the conduct of State Government, lest once more she should be untrue to herself.

But the question has to be put, Whether it be not the case that the Church has once again been untrue to herself ? Of course I refer to the many Church pronouncements, with their political Preambles, very important for explaining the Church Reform taken in hand, or the conferences and sessions lying behind these pronouncements. Yet the meaning of these Preambles, rather, was not the possibly justifiable affirmation, that by means of political events God's leading has now given a chance to the Church to give new heed and obedience to the Word of God, which is " The Church's One Foundation." Again, the meaning of these Preambles was not simply the *de facto* admission of the New State as the " Higher Power," co-ordinated with the Church by God, according to *Romans* xiii. Its meaning was merely a political opinion : one like that which disestablished the Church at the time of the victory of the Revolution of 1918. Then the Church rightly kept quiet. But does not the fact that to-day the Church has not kept quiet make her then rightful attitude suspect ? Was she mute then simply from the same considerations as those from which she deems she ought speak now ? The point is really not as to whether the men of the Church who, then by silence now by speaking, are to blame for expressing their political views as such, so far as they answer to their private convictions. But

26

who gave them the authority to express this opinion of theirs in the name of the Church ? to establish the Church anew upon their political views ? to "assimilate" (Gleichschaltung) Church and State on the Fundamental Article, and by this "assimilation" to exclude from the Church about-to-be-reformed those who do not agree with their opinions, and to bind the Church to one particular form of secular process in irresponsible fashion ?

And above all, in principle, to set the ball a-rolling for Church Reform by means of proclamations of a new and unheard-of rule of theological standard ? Or, is not this a proclamation of a new and unheard-of rule and standard in the Evangelical Church, when it is now publicly avowed that they have learnt to see the "new commission of the Lord to the Church," *not* at all in the Sacred Scriptures, *but* "in the great events of our days" ? Alongside of this, what may the clause mean, "Bound into the Word of God" ? "Bound into God's Word," the Church would remain in God's Word and would not hear the voice of a stranger. *Quo jure* did they proceed in quite a different manner ? For, would not anyone realise that in these preambles the Church had listened to the voice of a stranger, i.e. not to the voice of the Word of God, but to the voice of human judgment, merely political ? Without necessity from without, merely because she was not sure in herself of her task, because she did not *know* how to distinguish between theology and politics ? Because, out of political enthusiasm she did not *want* to distinguish ? At any rate, the Church *has* not distinguished, she was not true to her theme. And in this way, in the ambiguity, in the embarrassment in which the Church is always finding herself, when she might be a Church and yet forgets and is afraid to be a Church : *in this* way she has adopted the Reform-Movement. Then it was possible that the Reform-business might have been carried on with that solemnity, that spiritual assurance, which we feel is a-wanting to her. No one has the good conscience and the upright carriage requisite for such a work.

HOW THE CHURCH CAN RECTIFY HER FALSE STEP

By the above reference I do not intend to try and upset what has been done. Its later course can always be better than the start was. The mere fact that now, *hominum confusione et Dei providentia* (by the blundering of men and the providence of God), it has actually *begun* as a fact, *and* the other fact, that by the latest events it has actually been *checked* in its course,* may and should be an opportunity, like the whole of " the great events of our days," for the Church to enter upon the work of transforming herself externally, perhaps with real legitimacy. The new day with its new circumstances brings with it a new crisis, turning-point. Has not the glaring need of the Church, clamouring really for " reform in head and members," become patent for the first time, perhaps directly through this false step, or its consequence, which she took in the spring of this year? And, aware of the glaring need, should not the active forces and insights of the Church be requisitioned for ruling this reform ? Ought not God's Word and command, since till now perhaps we have been simply too arbitrary,

* Translator's note. The reference is to von Bodelschwingh's appointment as prospective *Reichs*-bishop ; the " German Christian " objection to him and preference for Army-Chaplain Mueller ; the Church protest against the latter, and von Hindenburg's expression of sympathy with that protest. Later, by the drastic changes in the voters' lists of members, Mueller was actually appointed Bishop of Prussia's State Church, and is now the *Reichs*-bishop.

C

to be *now* heard as commanding? And consequently, ought not Church *Reform* to issue forth
from out of the life of the Church itself, and thus
be capable of becoming real reform of the *Church*?
A lot of enthusiasm and seriousness has been put
into this business during the past months: but
the Holy Scriptures have not been allowed to be
the Master in this work, and, therefore, the Word
of God has not either. And yet the Evangelical
Church still possesses the Bible, and with it the
promise of reform, not by human, political and
Church-political arbitrariness, but by means of
the Word of God. Where the Bible is allowed to
be Master, theological existence is present: and
where theological existence lives, it is then possible
for Church reform to issue from the Church's life.
Where there is no theological existence, then, in
our own day, as in every age of the Church in which
she seeks selfishly to help herself, reform can and
will be still-born.

II—THE QUESTION OF ELECTING THE REICHS-BISHOP

The question which hitherto has characterised
the reform of the German Church above all else,

and which at once gave rise to the unlovely Church dispute was that of the *Bishop*. One can readily understand how later Church history has been bothered with the problem. What serious, inwardly significant, reasons were set out theologically so that in the Church movement of the year reckoned to be A.D. 1933 *this* question should have acquired importance, as is now the case? Lo! one day there was total unanimity, yes! on the whole line from Zoellner to Hossenfelder.* Then the conviction arose that the New Evangelical Church must above all, and in any case, become " free to elect," i.e. acquire, a Leadership, placed in the hands of one man, and that there should be in every one of the State Churches,† a State Bishop; and then, further, a Bishop for the whole nation, in whom the union of the several State Churches was to be organised and represented: in fact, a *Reichs*-Bishop. It was said, " We need and we want ' spiritual,' ' authoritarian ' Leaders, and finally and supremely, *one* spiritual, authoritative Leader."

* Note. The latter is a prominent " German Christian " leader, now appointed Bishop of Brandenburg; October, 1933.

† Translator's note. There are, or were, 29 separate States, each with its own " Landes-Kirche."

Here again the question arises, Did any one of us even so much as dream of the acute need for this theological conception of a National Bishop when this year came in ? To be sure, the notion of an Evangelical Church Bishop in Germany has had a long history. In most recent years the idea has been toyed with in Germany, and not without some partial result. But at the same time were we not quite satisfied that all the to-do about the attempted and partially successful bishop-making did not mean the introduction of an active office of a Bishop (i.e. like that of the Roman Catholic Bishop, having special ecclesiastical authority and dogmatic rule), but that by " Bishop " was merely meant a reference to the awkward term, " General Superintendent " : which is a somewhat more fitting designation—although not a Bishop at all as theology knows it, but simply an administrative term, indicating a person with the warrant to supervise in the larger districts of the country, and a person elevated to such office from among the ranks of common Evangelical Church clergy ?

The Bishop of 1933 was, and is, obviously, *not* this innocuous and titular Bishop. Had he been so, how would the shrillness of the cry for one :—

how, above all, could the fieriness imparted to the slogan, " Mueller or Bodelschwingh," be accounted for ? If the *Reichs*-Bishop had been the one thing necessary, and yet at the very start of the proceedings could be abandoned, and if the cry, " Mueller or Bodelschwingh " were so important as both parties asserted, then it is at once patent that this time, the intention of all those who wanted a Bishop at all, was to get a *real* Bishop. Yes! but one such as theology knows of : a real one, with pre-eminence, the holder of an ecclesiastical office differentiated from the offices held in the Church by ministers, elders, teachers and deacons : one equipped with the special prerogatives and with the appropriate special authority. In a word, a Bishop such as till now is only to be seen in Roman Catholic doctrines, but not in the doctrines of the Evangelical Church.

If they did *not* mean this kind of Bishop, but simply an ornate General Superintendent, such as perhaps is styled " Bishop " in the Anglican and Scandinavian Churches, then, in Germany to-day, where there is really no time nor strength for playing, those who shouted for a Bishop would have been spared the scarcely deserved epithet of " lightheadedness." In another respect, they partly deserve this reproach : they wanted, and set their hearts on getting, a real Bishop. They might drop calling themselves " light-headed," for later on they explained themselves as if, in fact, all that they had intended was a Bishop in the Anglican and Scandinavian sense of the term.

" BISHOP " AFTER THE HITLER PATTERN

The origin of the 1933 notion of Bishop is as plain as a pikestaff. " No imitation of State patterns ! " said Zoellner. " And yet," one may rejoin, " the whole of the business about the 1933 Bishop-question is beyond a doubt a copying of a definite ' Government pattern.' " In the political movement of this time there was present before men's gaze the impressive form of a Leader, who, by action, by the ability to seize political power and utilise it, had proved himself to be such. It was said, " The Church must have that kind of leader," and some men simply bolstered up this statement by urging " reasons of State," viz., " That a State under leadership can only have a similar kind of Church under leadership, alongside of and within itself." A second group, on the other hand, used this plea, that they too wanted to provide such a leadership to the Church, and they thought they would strengthen the Church as against the State. Yet again, there were others who now all at once found that the principle of leadership should be granted from the distinctive nature of the Church and on behalf of the Church itself, and be actualised within the Church itself.

Mark the word!—they meant the principle of leadership as seen in the concrete form of Adolf Hitler and leaders under him. What other kind of " leader " could men be thinking about, when, in the Germany of the spring of 1933, the word was on all men's lips? But when this " leadership principle " is translated into theological language, it discloses something that all the waters of the Rhine cannot wash away. And that is, the active, strict, Roman Catholic Prelacy. A Bishop is called for, even when no pains are taken, when the task of clearing up the idea to the mind is dodged : a magisterial Bishop, with the episcopal crozier, with which one can smite! A Bishop is called for, who, by virtue of some characteristic endowment, can watch over the authority of the

Creed, can watch, say, over the correct interpretation of Scripture within the Church, can
expose false doctrine, can be in a position to
overawe false doctrine with authority, with power
to appoint and dismiss ministers and professors,
with the authority to pass by and ignore the official
preachers and teachers as he makes his allocutions
directly to the Church, one to whom has been
remitted the function of presenting the proper
view of the Church in its relations with the
Government at home and with Churches of
other countries, in this or that matter as he
deems fit.

Moreover, if this was not intended, then the
proclamation of the Formula of the spiritual,
authoritarian Leader, and the outcry for the same,
would have shown a reprehensible lack of thought.
Again, in this respect at any rate, there was no
lack of thought : just this kind of Bishop was
intended, only—and here the question of " light-
mindedness " appears in quite a different aspect—
even the least of all those who clamoured so eagerly
for the Church " Leader," only needed to think
a bit, and, by translating into theological language
the word " leader "—a term stamped entirely by
the present-day political situation—could have

made clear to themselves what they definitely intended and desired. This most elementary step of theological reflection was omitted in the most enthusiastic eagerness to set about the building of this " tower."

More yet. They neglected what could not possibly have been omitted had they been awake to maintain the life of theology, and not gone to sleep theologically through their churchly political enthusiasm. Did no one particularly ask whether the imitating of a political method could at least be very suspicious in itself within and by the Church ? How sharp-eyed we were at one time in the persuasion that the establishment and organisation of the monarchical Episcopate upon the soil of the Ancient Church, corresponding to the Roman Empire, could be construed as a symptom of the secularising of that Church ! And now, as a matter of course, we have fixed this beam in our own eyes !

Yet more still. The following point has to be pondered. Real leading (the distinction between this term and that of ruling or conducting has indeed yet to be drawn), in all spheres where leading comes into consideration, can really only be certain as *event*. When the man is on the spot who in fact

37

leads, he exactly *is* the leader. I am also now thinking of Adolf Hitler.

Were I a National Socialist I would argue as follows against the talk now current about the Church "Leader," now to be appointed. I would say :—" We National Socialists did not think the office of a Leader was good or necessary. But Adolf Hitler was on the spot : the leader *led* and *was* one. He did not need an office, for in our Party it is not his superior charge that makes him to be a leader, or the office of Chancellor of the *Reich*, but because he *is* the leader, he has this charge, and was to be Imperial Chancellor through the victory of our Party. *This* is what should be copied within the Church. For then, and then alone, is there any sense in talking about a Church office of leadership. Neither Mueller nor Bodelschwingh, nor anybody else has till now copied him in this respect, *Ergo* . . . ."

LEADERSHIP DE FACTO

Why should there not be actual leadership within the Church ? But there would only be sense in speaking of it, even within the Church, if it were *actually there*. It *was* actual occurrence in the case of Luther and Calvin. In their case it was not in virtue of a special office—indeed, without their having later to become the bearers of such a special office—but simply within their usual office as preachers and professors in Wittenberg and Geneva that it was *recognised, granted* to them, to lead very authoritatively, very spiritually but, above all, very really. Were Luther and Calvin with us nowadays the " leadership principle " would have some meaning, and without the need for creating a special office of Bishop. But there is no sense in first providing and establishing a Church office of leadership in order to put someone into it, trusting that he may be capable of discharging its duties, even though one's confidence may be ever so well founded. Leadership is only present when it is *accomplished matter-of-fact*. The *principle* of leadership talked about is sheer nonsense. Whoever says otherwise does not know what he is talking about.

But even this pretext is not decisive. The question must now be asked, How does it come about that the cry for a Bishop, as for the authoritative spiritual leader, could ever have been possible, without those calling and those heeding the call, not feeling obliged to explain beforehand to themselves and others, whether and how far such an episcopal office might be *allowed* and *demanded* in the Evangelical Church at all ? As a matter of fact they have not explained, even in principle, to themselves what they assented to in connection with such a bishopric. The result is that anyone who opposes the project of a bishopric to-day runs the risk of finding some fine morning that he looks like Don Quixote. For any day it may be announced in public that no one ever thought of having a real Bishop, or maybe, that in future will ever think of such. Has theological confusion reached such a pitch in Evangelical Germany, that, at length, without incurring any risk, a favourite new doctrine can be coolly proclaimed, not only without authority, but without the ghost of a theological proof, simply because, for the sake of a Revolution, it pleases and in this way gets a footing ? The outcome is (in this respect not within the Reformed Church, i.e. Calvinist), not only does no one ask for a theological proof—in revolutionary times there is no time for theological reflection—but everybody feels quite convinced that all will be right with the new doctrine !

And has even any one single responsible official explained the grotesque feature of the business of proceeding to the *election* of a Bishop and a sorry *fight* about him, without having previously *defined*, at least doctrinally and in order according to Church law, what is intended and expected of such a Bishop (if, in its hurry, theological proof were to be discarded), so that the Church could wait comfortably to see what content the new office would acquire through its occupant ?—so that the friends of the Bishop would not know aforehand that he could only be a somewhat ornate General Superintendent like the Anglican or Swedish " Bishop," without fullness of power and authority in doctrine ? What a lack of seriousness there has been in this playing with the matter ! Is it astonishing that the strife that has happened, as to who shall be National Bishop, with such a background to set it off, has made the Evangelical Church look ridiculous ? The consequences may turn out to be worse than all the actual and imagined evil of the past, which it was thought would and could be remedied with a National German Church and a National Bishop.

THE REFORMED (CALVINIST) CHURCH ATTITUDE TO THE BISHOP QUESTION

I see no way out of this *cul de sac* except the road back. Stop playing and be serious ! We of the Reformed Church have at least done so. We took with gravity and in a theological manner the announcement of an authoritarian Bishop, and we gave our reason theologically for most decidedly refusing such. We said that the office of Chief Pastor, the sovereignty and authority of Jesus Christ or of the Holy Scriptures, can have its counterpart within the Church only within the ministry of the ordained officers of the separate churches in the Synodal Union, when mutually admonishing, confirming, or disallowing one another, but not in the special office of a bishop ranked in order superior to the officers of the various churches. We declared that we hoped for the leading of the Church as a whole—that is to say, as the *One* Church in the *several* churches—so far as we expect it at all from man, only from the authorised ministry in the churches, but we could not look for it from the episcopal throne set up *ad hoc*. This declaration, at any rate, is plain enough.

THE LUTHERAN CHURCH ATTITUDE TO THE BISHOP QUESTION

We have looked in vain, till now, for a similarly expounded and reasoned counter-statement. We supposed that there might perhaps be a parallel statement of the *Lutheran Church's* theology, for, to us, the so-called " Bishop-idea " till now was particularly admitted to be a postulate of our comrades in the faith of the Lutheran persuasion. But till now this statement, the Evangelical Church *locus de episcopo*—the doctrine concerning the actual Evangelical Bishop—has not been laid on the table by any of the present holders of the office of Lutheran Bishop, or even Erlangen, Goettingen, Leipzig, Rostock, or any other of the chief academical centres of Lutheranism, whether to prove or even to formulate it. What more important work could have been done in those places, and ultimately, in every Lutheran parsonage, if it were at all necessary for Lutheranism to set up an actual Bishop ? And in the same respect, how, if the new doctrine should turn out to be still incompatible with Lutheran theology ? What the now removed " designated *Reichs*-Bishop," Dr. von Bodelschwingh, said and did, during his active period as such—I have in mind especially his published Pastoral Epistle at Whitsuntide—was an abrogation and negation of the real Bishop. In every line he was an Evangelical Christian and theologian keeping to the Word : in no line the authoritarian spiritual leader. God be praised that it was so ! And God be praised

43

that now beforehand he has been graciously preserved to become, yea, must be, in future an
authoritative ecclesiastical leader! But should it
not have been an important duty for Dr. von
Bodelschwingh, first of all, to learn and tell us
whether, and in what respect, he was disposed for
a period of time to write Pastoral Epistles (which
were *not* Pastoral Epistles), whether there should
and must be in the Evangelical Church an actual
Bishop at all, disposed to lead by such and the like
actions? But whoever he be that henceforth
thinks of demanding the actual Bishop and defend-
ing and even *being* Bishop, he is herewith invited
to define and indicate this actual Bishop theologically! Not sociologically, not politically, not
by a philosophy of history or of Tillich's " Kairos,"
but theologically by means of Scripture and the
Confessional Creed! *Or else*, he should explain in
proper form, that the establishment of a real
Bishop's office beneath the allusion to the notion of
" leader " that dominates to-day, has been dropped;
that all the grandiose words that have been uttered
(again, on the whole line of Churchmen from
Zoellner to Hossenfelder!) must, from now on, be
speech in defiance towards one who will be an
administrative, ornamental holder of a " bishopric,"

who has *no* authority as regards doctrine, worship
and Church constitution, who can*not* appoint or
dismiss ministers, and so on. But so long as no one
will openly give a statement in one sense or the other
of what " bishop " means, can this whole business
of creating and electing a *Reichs*-Bishop be described
otherwise than as a colossal blunder ? A blunder in
which the Church (and the likelihood of it has
never been contradicted) has acted in a way that
is worldly in principle, because of her quite uncalled-
for enthusiasm or fearfulness to " assimilate " herself to the Government of the day. And can anything else be said but this, that it is high time for
the Church to become self-controlled again, sober
to the recognition that the German Evangelical
Church, so far as she is in the One, Holy, Universal
Church, *has* the " Leader " in Jesus Christ, the Word
of God, Who can provide her with human " leaders "?
So that precisely for this reason—and, to-day, just
as thoroughly as Israel of yore had to on Mount
Carmel—the German Evangelical Church has to
make up her mind whether she is content with *His*
leading, and with *His* ability to supply us with
leaders. Or, whether along with the Church of the
Pope, and as a poor copy of her, because trusting
in an arm of flesh, she is wilfully to commit

45   D

her destinies into the custody of a self-elected leader.

The German Evangelical Church, through her responsible respresentatives, has not comported herself as the Church which *possesses* her Leader, during these recent months. And yet *H*e possesses *her* : as surely as we have to hear His law and His Gospel ever again from Him. When it is recognised that *He*, and *He alone*, is the Leader, there is the possibility of theological existence. And then, in all deference, even if one be but an ever-so-insignificant theologian, or the obscure village pastor, or even not a pastor or theologian at all, but " merely " somebody like a lay-elder, then one is *himself* the genuine Bishop, if he only knows his Bible and his Catechism : a " bishop " as foreseen in Holy Writ. Where there is no theological life about ; when men *call out* for the Church leader instead of themselves *being* leaders in their appointed ministries ; then all this crying out for a leader is as vain as the howling of the priests of Baal on Carmel, " Baal, hear us ! "

III—ON THE " GERMAN CHRISTIANS "

The so-called " Faith-movement of German Christians " is entitled to the renown, for what it is worth, of having ushered into existence the Reform of the German Church in 1933, and not least the Bishop question. From several quarters I have been asked why I made no public utterance against this Movement. Why till now I have not spoken is simply because what I have to say on this topic was sufficiently obvious : anyone who knows me but slightly could say it just as well himself. But there have been some doubts as to this obviousness. Certain members of the Reformed Church (Calvinist) with whom I collaborated during the last few months, and also some who have passed as being pupils of mine, have appeared in the ranks of the " German Christians." The obviousness can now be stated plainly. Emphatically and distinctly but, yet only *en passant* I say it, because what I say about them seems to be necessary as paving the way for what I have to say at the appearance of the " German Christians."

First of all as to the aims of the " German Christians." I follow their directions as presented

47

in two admittedly standard documents, of equal
importance, of dates May 5th and 16th last. Their
guiding rule and purpose, viewed from the theological standpoint, runs thus :

" It seems to us," they say, " that the German
people, reflecting on the deepest springs of its life
and power, wants to return to Church. Therefore,
the German Churches have to do everything so
that this may come to pass." The Church has to
prove herself to be the Church for the German
people because " she helps the people to understand
and fulfil the vocation entrusted to it by God," as
this is " the ultimate purpose of the present Government." Consequently, the German Churches also
must acquire a constitution, " making them capable
of rendering service to the German people entrusted to them by the Gospel of Jesus Christ."
This is exactly what the " German Christians " are
acquiring. But what distinguishes these " German
Christians " and their demands, in view of other
demands which perhaps sound a similar note ?
This :—to them the acknowledgment of " the
majesty of the National Socialist Government "
is not only a matter of citizenship, but also a matter
of religious belief, and they demand a Church
that agrees with them in this. According to them,
the Gospel in future must be preached as " The

Gospel in the Third Reich."* The Credal confession must be preserved, but it must be expanded in the sense of " a fierce attack against Mammonism, Bolshevism and un-Christian pacifism." In future the Church must be " the Church of the German people," that is to say " of Christians of the Aryan race." The *Reichs*-Bishop as " spiritual leader who has to be responsible personally for the ruling decisions," is to be elected by " primary ballot and by the voting lists of ' German Christians ' " ; non-Aryan Christians being excluded from voting.

In a later notification a third test is applied: the Bishop is to be a man enjoying the special confidence of the Imperial Chancellor (A. Hitler). What is the Church to do about her Creed ? The reply is : " The Church is to supply us with the weapons for the war against all non-Christian principles, and such principles as may corrupt the nation." And how is this to be brought about ? Thus :—" The training and guidance of the ministry of the Church need a radical transformation to bring them closer to ordinary life, and to make a closer connection with the community," etc. etc.

* Translator's note. " Third Reich," their slogan, refers to the first Empire under Charlemagne, a thousand years and more ago : then, to the German Empire, the name given after the Franco-German War of 1870 : now, the Hitler *Régime*. It has affinities with the Puritan " Third Kingdom," the " reign of the saints."

DR. BARTH'S OPPOSITION TO " GERMAN CHRISTIAN " DOCTRINES

What I have to say to all this is simply said. I say, absolutely and without reserve, NO ! to both the spirit and the letter of this doctrine. I maintain that this teaching is alien, with no right, in the Evangelical Church. I maintain that the end of that Church will have come if this teaching ever comes to have sole sway within her borders, as the " German Christians " intend that it shall. I maintain that the Evangelical Church ought rather to elect to be thinned down till it be a tiny group and go into the catacombs than make a compact, even covertly, with this doctrine. I maintain that those who have come to terms with this teaching are either seduced or seducers, and I can only recognise in this " Faith-Movement " the Church and features such as I am forced to recognise even in the Roman Papacy. I have a request to make to my various theological friends also, who find themselves shifted into being in a position to say Yes ! to this teaching, having been " doped " or tricked by some sophism. I ask them to take note from me, that I feel myself utterly and finally divided from them, save so far as, by a lucky inconsistency, there may be retained by them some yet solid core of what is Christian, churchly and theological, alongside of this heresy. I offer the following as the reasons for my refusal of them.

1. The Church has not " to do everything " so that the German people " may find again the way into the Church," but so that *within* the Church the people may find the Commandment and promise of the free and pure Word of God.

2. It is not the Church's function to help the German people to recognise and fulfil any one " vocation " different from the " calling " from and to Christ. The German people receives its vocation from Christ to Christ through the Word of God to be preached according to the Scriptures. The Church's task is the preaching of the Word.

3. Speaking generally, the Church has not to be at the service of mankind, and so, not of the German people. The German Evangelical Church is the Church with reference to the German people : she is only in service to the Word of God. It is God's will and work, if by means of His Word mankind, and of course, the German people, are ministered unto.

4. The Church believes in the Divine institution of the State as the guardian and administrator of public law and order. But she does not believe in any State, therefore not even in the German one, and

therefore not even in the form of the National Socialistic State. The Church preaches the Gospel in all the kingdoms of this world. She preaches it also *in* the Third *Reich*, but not *under* it, nor in *its* spirit.

5. If the Church's Confession of Faith is to be expanded it must be according to the standard of Holy Scripture, and not at all according to the examples, positive or negative, of a view of things existing at some one particular period of time, be it a political philosophy, or otherwise. Therefore, she must not widen the Creed to include the National Socialists' " world-view." Nor has the Church to " provide weapons " for " us," or any one whatever.

6. The fellowship of those belonging to the Church is not determined by blood, therefore, not by race, but by the Holy Spirit and Baptism. If the German Evangelical Church excludes Jewish-Christians, or treats them as of a lower grade, she ceases to be a Christian Church.

7. *If* the office of a *Reichs*-Bishop should be possible at all, then that office, like every other Church office, must not be established according to political programmes and methods at all. That is to say, methods of primary elections, political programmes, etc., but by the representatives of the regular administration within the Churches, from the point of view of what exclusively empowers him for a *Church* office.

8. Not " in the sense of a closer approach to life and connection with the community " is " the

training and leading of the ministry to be trans-
formed " (as the Faith-Movement declares), but
on the lines of a stricter, broader education, with
pith and substance for the development of the work
solely charged upon pastors, viz. the work of
preaching the Word according to Scripture.

9. . . . . *

Without making any claim to completeness these
are some of the tenets to be advocated against the
" German Christians." But although I may advocate
them so emphatically, I would not have taken to
the platform simply to repel the " German Christians " ; and I expect absolutely nothing at all
from any discussion with their spokesmen. To be
sure, their growth and increase is a reason for
anxiety. Still, I would not have " taken the floor "
as if a heresy, that had never raised its head before
with them, had popped up. Oh dear, no! The
veriest tyro in theology knows that with their thinking we are dealing with a small collection of odds
and ends from the great theological dust-bins (this
happy phrase is not mine ; I've borrowed it) of
the despised eighteenth and nineteenth centuries.
Nor would I have spoken because they have a

* Note. (Here Dr. Barth leaves a line starred. The next
sentence may explain why.)

53

dangerous skill and power of spirit when pushing their doctrines !

No ! but at last simply because they have shown, and still show, that there can be a " Faith-Movement " which even possesses form and force by using violence after the manner of political mass demonstrations and forced recruiting campaigns. That a scholarly pastoral conference, with a purely scholarly report is made incapable of meeting, because some ministers, who are opposed to the reporter politically, simply threaten with interruption—all this, to be sure, is quite original and marvellous ! That Luther's grand hymn, " Eine feste Burg ist unser Gott " (" A sure stronghold our God is He ") can be sung to the accompaniment of the rumble of military drums : that the slogan, " Peasants, capture the Churches ! " is made possible —this also is new and alarming ! And if one pays heed to their naming of theological opponents publicly, and calling them " coteries without a Fatherland," as " those sour-faced parsons," who within two years (i.e. after the release of the Saar region from the control of the International Commission) will get " not simply *one* blow of the *cudgel* " (I'm not quite sure which word is to be underlined), then this is something picturesque and

54

new, and can easily lead on to becoming something dangerous to life. But when it is publicly
manifested as an essential feature of this " Faith
Movement " that it agitates at this low level, then
it is so threatening that it is certainly more discreet
not to enter into disputation with it, but to give it,
or at least its leaders, the go-by, and address one's
remarks to other folk.

What I mean is this, that we have more urgent
and more important things to occupy our attention
than those have who want to contradict and give
theological instruction to the " German Christians."
However bad they may be, it seems to me that
far worse has been the attitude till now that the
Evangelical Church has adopted by entering into
engagements with them. If the German Evangelical
Church had been in a healthy condition things here
would have turned out differently. What, then,
has happened ?

" EVANGELICAL CHURCH " ATTITUDES

On the side of the Church this has happened. A
point-blank amazing lack of resistance, in which
pastors and church members, professors and students
of theology, educated and illiterate, old and young,

Liberals, Fundamentalists and Pietists, Lutherans and Calvinists, have surrendered in droves at the noise of this Movement : surrendered as one falls under the spell of a real, downright psychosis. Those of one group yield in honest belief that they have now heard a direct Messianic Gospel. Another group capitulates with something of very deep thought on philosophical lines, for it is supposed that one becomes most assured if he allows himself to be overtaken and captured most radically by " Reality " ! A third section surrenders through simply considering that what is all right in the political arena will surely be just and fair on the floor of the Church. A fourth party, fearful lest they be shunted into a siding and, consequently, their noble talents run to waste, swim with the stream, for all " runs one way." The fifth group " give in," with shrewd circumspection, giving assent only to " the good " in the Movement : a sixth section goes aside with hesitating gait, in order to form, as soon as may be, " the necessary Opposition," " to overcome from inside the one-sidedness " of the Movement. But one and all surrender to a cause which bears so distinctly on its brow the brand of topsy-turvydom.

That already a candidate for confirmation has

had to take note, that in a healthy Church he cannot remain alone for a single hour, with either the Lutheran or the Heidelberg Catechism in his hand, and get on with it, under any pretext! And those who have *not* joined up with the Movement have often thought, that this could be taken with such deadly seriousness, and they would not indeed be unfair to it. Yet they could lay none too little emphasis upon the personal sincerity and zeal of many of this Movement's leaders and followers, which, by the way, even I certainly may not doubt, and they ought to be glad at the "life" that has so unexpectedly come into the Church. In brief : those *not* joining up thought they would show that they were not narrow-minded, but were quite open to all that was new and honest : that not only did they see in this Movement something new but true as well, and therefore they felt that they must regard the "faith" of this "Faith Movement" in future as something at least most worthy of discussion.

Where in all this was the plain but critical question as to Christian *truth* : When could all this be possible ? Or, is it that this question dare not be put at all in the present Evangelical Church ? Has the quest for truth been totally suppressed in one jubilation or groaning by the shouts of Revolution, Reality, Life, Mastery of Destiny! and all those other bombastic slogans that stifle all Christian criticism? Has one to be dubbed a stiff-backed ecclesiastic or a dry-stick from a student's den if he permits himself to hold that the rowdiest drum-taps as such are not, in the long run, any *argument* at all? Is the " fine thing " in the Movement perhaps this, that thousands never openly asked first of all as regards it: What is the Christian truth? But if all this should be true at all, how profoundly and solidly we should have stayed in the " Faith Movement" of the eighteenth and nineteenth centuries! For this is where its highest truth lay : " never to allow the request for, and answer for, aught of truth to be made in the Church, for it would only lead to strife and intolerance, and because nothing could be settled concerning truth and untruth, but ' life ' alone would matter ! "

CRITICISM OF THE " COMMITTEE OF THREE " AT LOCCUM AND BERLIN CONFERENCES

Here I feel constrained to speak a frank word about the proceedings at Loccum and Berlin. In a healthy Church, such as the Evangelical Church should be, it ought not to have been possible that the " Faith Movement " of the " German Christians," in the person of one of those responsible for the combined errors of this Party, should have been admitted to the official collaborations at the drafting of the Confession and Constitution of the Church. I am aware, and allow for, the fact that Army Chaplain Mueller, as the Imperial Chancellor's " confidential man," *had* to be admitted to these conferences. In principle there is nothing to be said against that, for the Government has the claim to be represented officially in this matter. Though it should have been an understood thing, that along with the presence of the State's representative, sessions for abundant talks of the Church Commissioners, *between themselves*, ought to have been very carefully seen to. But the impossible actually happened. The " Committee of Three," instead of treating the Government's representative with the regard his function requires, within due limits, to inspect its work and provide opportunities for communicating the Government's desires and opinions, went beyond this. They took upon themselves, as if a matter of course, to welcome Chaplain Mueller as a fourth member into their conclave, and, as was aptly said, " to sit with them at the Board at ' the confidential collaboration.' " (If the grave objections to the theology of the State representative, which in this instance were in existence, had not needed to be cleared away, this ought not to have occurred.) Army Chaplain Mueller was regarded as being a man of tender, religious piety : I do not question it. But this ought not to have made any difference, or presented any difficulty, for the Church Committee to have explained frankly to him, or in any case to the Chancellor (A. Hitler) who had sent him, that in his quality as " Protector " of the " German Christians," he could not be heard at all as a *theologian*, nor could he expect to acquire any influence within their circle.

The fruit of Mueller's co-operation can be plainly seen in the Confession of Faith which issued from Loccum. As now published it is so intolerable, from a theological point of view. And, on account of its defects and ambiguities, it will remain a document, in any case, to take no pride in, even if certain corrections were to be run through it—a thing little likely to take place, when one considers the latest turn of events. Did the Committee of Three feel obliged to act in this way out of regard for the Chancellor ? It is indeed a moot question whether the latter's intention, when sending Herr Mueller, was to force the theology of the " German Christians " upon the German Evangelical Church, and whether he would not rather have been glad to have obtained on this occasion a clear explanation of what that Church is, and is not. Or, was the theology of the " Three " themselves so constituted that, as the conversations went on with Chaplain Mueller, no reference was made concerning his theological character, and that, as the Loccum Confession shows, they could listen to him ? However it be, where, in this business, remains the Church's responsibility ? Where, too, at this place, the inevitability of the inquiry as to Christian Truth ?—an inevitability which could not be affected by any " brotherly love," so as to give scope and currency within the Church to this error. In view of the remarkable flabbiness with which the Church has been meeting the " German Christians," even in the Supreme Court of the Church itself, can anyone marvel at what the transaction has come to mean in the churches up and down the country ?

THE OPPOSITION FROM THE " NEW REFORMATION " MOVEMENT

The other matter that creates misgiving is the widespread and open *opposition* the " German Christian " Movement *also* has had to encounter in view of its incursion. There is a smaller and less public opposition for which the Church may be thankful. But if anyone is grateful for this, and would like to strengthen its influence as much as he can, such an one would have as much reason for being on guard against much, far too much, that has been said and done, as *against* the " German Christians " themselves. I am thinking of the " *New Reformation Movement.*" As authoritative documents explaining the nature and programme of this body, I may refer to their Appeals, of date May 9th and 18th ; and a Memorandum signed by Lic. Dr. Kuenneth, which I received on June 23rd, dealing with the Bishop question. The reasons why I cannot regard the opposition supplied by this Movement as legitimate and promising, as against the " German Christians," are the following :—

They are not standing out as an opposition based

on principle according to a Church theology which can be taken seriously. They grant in addition that the " German Christians " have given " the strongest impetus towards a radical re-organisation of the German Evangelical Church " ; further, they think that a large number of the " German Christians' " demands are " thoroughly justified." At first, their coming on the stage was interpreted both by themselves and others as " an action in support of the ' Committee of Three's ' work, inclusive of Chaplain Mueller." They felt that, " they were one with the ' German Christians ' in the desire for radical reform." They could " to a very large extent identify themselves with " the Manifestos of the moderate East Prussian wing of this movement, and " were in sympathy with it." On May 16th, when the new Regulations of the " German Christians " were published, drafted afresh according to the East Prussian wing's way of thinking, the New Reformers, along with so many others, were simple enough to assume that it was no longer necessary to take up an attitude of conflict against the new Policy that Movement had adopted ; indeed, they thought their leading ought to be met with confidence and that now they ought to be ready to co-operate with the Movement.

Later on, however, they were forced to confess that " the new programme of the ' German Christians ' exhibits a disastrous theological obscurity." But in the midst of the Bishop-question which had now come upon the scene, they explained that their entrance in support of Bodelschwingh's candidature did not mean in any way an opposition to the person of Army-Chaplain Mueller, whose importance for re-organisation of the Church they would not at all deny. It is now worthy of note that, in differentiation from the " German Christians," the New Reformers rejected the idea of excluding non-Aryans from the Church. And this is pre-eminently praiseworthy ; they inscribed on their banners the slogan : " The re-organisation of the Church from within the Church's nature " (Ger. Wesen). But *what* precisely has to be understood by the words, " nature of the Church " ?— particularly when occurring in an appeal to which, among others, are appended the signatures of such theologians as Heim, Gogarten, von Tiling, Jacobi, Lilje, Brunstaedt, Knak, Luetgert, Ritter, George Schulz, Schreiner, W. Staehler, combined with the expressed declaration that " The New Reformation Movement proclaims within its own ranks *public peace* " ? Of *what* nature of the Church are they cognisant, when they have admitted that they are in sympathy, co-operation, etc., also with a wing of the " German Christians," and have let themselves be misled by that body's new programme (differing not a hair's breadth in the points that are decisive), and have been put into a yet profounder slumber ? What does the phrase, " To work from the nature of the Church " mean, if, with reference to the Church's mission, in combination with the " joyous assent to the New German State " they proceed so thoughtlessly and secularly as the " Committee of Three " did, or any similar conference of ministers of the Church with a less glorious name ?

The New Reformers were among the most enthusiastic for a new office of *Reichs*-Bishop being created, and they were the most impatient for the nomination of one. In this they saw " a symbolical act of fresh Church unity," and they styled the demand for this symbolical action as their " Immediate Programme." On the ground of *which* conception, of *which* nature, of *which* Church ? " The arbitrariness of preaching must be dissolved by a fixed authority of doctrine." Can the authority of *that* doctrine really be meant which has permitted or bidden such a series of thoughtless items to the New Reformation Movement ? Ought

65

one, who is sitting himself in this way within a hot-house, really to be called upon to fight so hotly " the attempts of a ' liberal ' theology to penetrate again into the Church ? " And ought he to be called upon to defend the Church against the " German Christians " ? Perhaps he may be, to-morrow morning, when they have shed some of their radicalism ; perhaps he may be in a position to accompany them anew to brotherly collaboration ! Is not, or was not, the New Reformation Movement perhaps merely the successor of the old " Mediation Theology " in its occasional, but very spasmodical, battle waged against the old " Liberals " ? If one gives heed to all that the New Reformers adduced, according to their own declarations, as fighters for Bodelschwingh's candidature against the " German Christians " ; and in the Bishopric contest, really, what is there left remaining as the object of the contest but the idea of the formal independence of the Church as regards the State and political influences, which the New Reformers rightly regarded as threatened by the " German Christians " and Mueller's candidature ? I do not need to repeat what I have said against the " German Christians."

66

THE RELATIONS OF CHURCH AND STATE :
DR. BARTH'S FORECAST

At this point I can supplement what has preceded by stating how I reckon up the position of things as they are likely to eventuate. After the latest events I am more convinced than before. My view is, that a union with the Evangelical German Church which in any way has surrendered to Mueller and the " German Christians " will probably not be maintained. Disobedience will have to be rendered to the doctrines, *pronunciamentos*, and measures of the " German Christian " *Reichs*-Bishop and his prebendaries, which measures are to be expected as opposed to the Gospel. If necessary, even against them, the final consequences will have to be paid. And all this, even though 99 per cent. of those hitherto " Evangelical " Germans should attach themselves to the " German Christians." But please note : not on account of what divides the " New Reformers " from the " German Christians " will we pay the price of disobedience. These " New Reformers " are only in disagreement with the " German Christians " as regards the formal independence or dependence of the Church, but do *not* disagree concerning the nature of the Church. When it was said during the Bishop controversy that, for the sake of the Church, Bodelschwingh, and not Mueller, must be *Reichs*-Bishop, it was not true : at least, not true on the lips of the " New Reformers." For, if the point in question had been as to the nature of the Church, then, by all the evidence of the names appended to their Appeal, and in accord with the attitude stated in their own documents, they could just as well have voted for Mueller as for Bodelschwingh. In order to have particular importance the demand for an independent Church must contain a positive, confessional, theological content. This, at any rate, was lacking in the mouths of the New Reformation men. The demand of the " German Christians " for a Church *not* independent had, and has, such a content. This fact cannot be gainsaid, whatever we may care to think of it. Over against this content, the insistent struggle for Bodelschwingh, which was intended to be interpreted only as a " symbolical act," which simply *indicated* Church independency, could scarcely have achieved its purpose, and could not possibly have had any prospect of success, because of its unreality. "In this Sign" only fruitless Church-politics can be carried on. That is to say, Church-politics without substance from the spiritual, theological standpoint. Such Church-politics must exhaust itself by tactics against tactics, tricks and counter-tricks, pronouncement against pronouncement, as was seen clearly enough both before, during, and after the anything but edifying Ascension-tide in Berlin. On account of its form, such a Church-politics would have shown whether it might not have concealed a goodly portion of common politics, even as the opponents' politics usually does. Anyhow, both these opponents of yesterday come alike from the calamitous theology of the nineteenth century. As architects of a serious reconstruction of the Church neither of them should have been called in. But while, on the one hand, theological Modernism is clearly to be grasped as present in the " German Christians," and, as for example, in the statement made with reference to "non-Aryans," it is evident of itself: on the other hand, the New Reformation Men, with their three-fold cry, " The Temple of the Lord is here" (*Jer.* vii. 4, Luther's version), had so hidden theological Modernism behind their vociferous anti-Liberalism, that one could easily make the mistake of thinking *they* were *the* righteous among the unrighteous : in reality they were not. While the " German Christians," with a terrifying frankness made themselves out as being the defenders of the " Nation " called upon to " capture the Church," or as carrying out the logic of the dominating idea of the State ; the New Reformation Men, as the valiant defenders of the Church's freedom, seemed to have merited the applause of all who, as a matter of course, to a certain extent, " are well aware of what a Church is " beforehand ! While the apparently successful case of a victory for the " German Christians " appears to present to us a sort of " Age of Terror," seen from the theological view-point—(in which there will be a drumming to the worship of God, and in which E. Hirsch* will define what theology is !)—in the event of a victory falling to the New Reformation Movement, it would only result in a new, perpetual adjustment and compromise (Creation *and* Redemption, Nature *and* Grace, Nationalism *and* Gospel), which of yore has ever been more congenial to the " natural " man, than the characteristic solution which Christianity gives. My belief

* Editor of the *Theologische Litteraturzeitung*, and Professor at Goettingen.

is that at not too remote a time the Church will have finished with the public, savage heretics ; but who will have saved her from the blandishment of those who seem to be correct as to the standards of Church, Bible and Reformation, and yet, in principle do not think differently from those heretics ?

DR. BARTH MEETS ANTICIPATED CRITICISM OF HIS ATTITUDE

I am quite clear that with what I have said I may seem to have uttered many a hard saying, and to many who, till yesterday, honestly thought it was their duty to enrol under the banner of the New Reformation Party, prepared to do their part on behalf of the truly important subject of Church independency of the State. And it is probable that in the altered situation, with all integrity, they may seek deliverance by similar endeavours. Their course of reasoning is something like this.

" We stand in great peril of having a State-Church (Cæsaro-Papal) like that of the Age of Charlemagne, and again of the eighteenth century.

If this happens, then it will outwardly and automatically be all over with liberty of preaching and of theology. For then a different Gospel from that of ' The Gospel in the Third *Reich* ' will simply have been suppressed by machinery. Then the Churches will be famished and infected. The liability is therefore laid upon us : we are responsible for the Church and have to ward off this peril. And now, *what*-ever and *who*-ever can help, let him do so ! Fancy ! a dry-stick-of-the-study laying down conditions ! Something must and has to be done. Yesterday a front was constructed, like that of the New Reformation Men, of necessity. And to-day, something like it becomes necessary also." So they think.

I understand this train of thought quite well, but I think it is all wrong. It is not serious enough, and in the Churches now, and indeed, to-day more than yesterday, nothing but serious thought should obtain. The liberty of preaching and of theology, which is now to be guarded, cannot consist primarily in making safe against the external, machine-like oppression by the " German Christians," which is to be anticipated. The liberty that has to be preserved is *liberty* : and by liberty I mean the sovereignty of the Word of God in preaching and theology. We cannot make too clear to ourselves that *this* liberty or sovereignty, according to the history of the past two centuries from which we all derive, is not a matter-of-fact thing : that we are not at all secured directly on this side, even though we might for so long have been fully secured against the eruption and the threatening from without by " German Christians." This eruption itself can be a clearest final signal of how the liberty, that is, the sovereignty, of the Word of God within the Church of Evangelical Germany, has, as a whole, been *for a long while* and quite *generally* threatened. Along with the external oppression of the Church she can be summoned to consider that God is at liberty to take away the light of the Gospel, if we do not want to have it otherwise. Even as He once removed the " candlestick " from the North African Church, which was as much the Church of St. Augustine as the German Church is that of Luther. It would then be a fruitless and a silly thing to fight, by means of the instruments of Church-politics, against the sign given us in maybe one last moment in which all that mattered would be to cry aloud unto God, in the presence of this certainly fearful signal, that He might not be altogether weary of His rule amidst the great

73

disloyalty of modern German Christianity and " Churchianity," and that He might be disposed to make us more loyal to His Word, by means of His Word, than we and our fathers have been.

It can even be so, in that case, and then the threatening machine-like persecution by the " German Christians," together with the peril of spiritual famine and corruption threatening us from that quarter, must be less feared than the danger that from us—yes, *us*, who are *not* " German Christians "—unless we turn right round, the Word of God may be taken away. And it might be the case that a very different battle enlist us : a conflict having nothing to do with pollings and placards and protests, with mobilisations and " fronts " : a battle not *about* but *within* the Church, not for *protecting* but by *practising* of preaching and of theology : not *against* the " German Christians " but even implicitly with and exactly *for* them : a struggle in which we cannot expect to win, but can only hope to be forced to yield. But now, like Jacob, to yield, and by so doing, right away thus *be* an Evangelical Church.

" Let *what*-ever and *who*-ever can help, do

so!"? "Public peace" with any man, if only he
be on our side against the threatening State
Churchianity? NO! This no longer holds. The
whole of Church-politics and its powers and prospects would then be far away. In a trice, the
anxiety because of the "German Christians," and
their possible and already won successes, would
have been removed instantly and thoroughly.
Partly because we were not at all engaged with
them, and partly because we were taken in with
their error and the power of their error, which, at
any moment, can be scattered like chaff to all the
winds that blow. In tranquillity and with joyful-
ness we should then be able to reflect upon their
power as on "The Gates of Hell" which of a surety
will not prevail against the Church. There would
then be no talk about all being favourable if Church-
politics won, or of all being lost if it were defeated.
And then we would only have to make common
cause with such as we had discovered in the common
travail for the Word of God. Nor would we join
hands with them in order to bring a new Movement, or a united "front" again, on to the field,
but in order that we might labour together
with them onward and yet onward in concern
for the Word of God. In this way, perhaps,

there might even be created a centre of resistance, which, because unsought, might one of these days possess an outstanding " political " importance for the Church ; and be effective against the danger impending over the Church to-day.

THE NEED TO-DAY : A SPIRITUAL CENTRE OF RESISTANCE

The *prime* need of our time is for a *spiritual* centre of resistance : one that would, for the first time, give a meaning and a content to Church politics. The man who understands this will not " gird himself for any fight," but will put on his programme, " WORK AND PRAY."

Now, let no one say too hastily : " This is no good to-day, amid the worries and disturbances of the summer of 1933." There are some theologians who ought to hang down their heads with shame for having preached such fine sermons on " God is our only Helper " (Psalm xlvi. ; Luther's rendering) and then snapping out " It's no good now." They should let the word come home to themselves that : " The help of the Lord is really the only help ; indeed, the only *real-politik* of help to the Church." And this help we can seek in the " MOMENT,"* and, to speak frankly, they are bound nowadays to seek it with new, absolutely serious, concern. Again, let no one say too hastily that in the concrete situation in which the Churches are now placed, something has to be done, altogether different from what has here been suggested, in order to stop the mischief. Of course something has to be done ; very much so ; but most decidedly nothing other than this, viz. that the Church congregations be gathered together again, but aright and anew in fear and great joy, to the Word by means of the Word. All the crying about and over the Church will not deliver the Church. Where the Church *is* a Church she is already delivered. Let persecution

---

* Translator's note. This is one of Dr. Barth's terms to express the " flash " of revelation. Browning's lines are the best exposition of the term :—

" . . . moments. When the spirit's true endowments
Stand out plainly from its false ones,
And apprise it if pursuing
Or the right way or the wrong way,
To its triumph or undoing."

—Cristina.

be never so severe, it will not affect her! "*Still*," it is said, "*still*, shall the City of God abide, lusty beside her tiny stream" (Psalm xlvi. 5 ; Luther's translation).

Let no one say in haste that with this advice the entire Church that is in jeopardy has been forgotten. As though the fate of the whole Church were settled in Berlin! As though you could exist spiritually within your quiet room and in pastoral activity so that, when the whole Church is at stake, you simply defend the spiritual in a worldly way! The whole Church is always " where two or three are gathered together unto the Name." Repeat and affirm the Creed of the Church by word and deed, where the Foe comes into sight in concrete form. Let it be repeated and affirmed also in the community of the Churches when this community is truly one of faith and not the community of a Church-political movement! Where the Creed is, the One, Holy Church is there present in the fight with error in which she will never lose the day. But, on the other hand, there is always error where there are " Movements," and divisions are ever nigh at hand. The Holy Ghost needs no " movements " ; the Devil has probably invented most of them.

78

So let no man tell me that I am attacking from behind the brave souls who, breathlessly, are standing for the Church on the line of the New Reformation, because I point out this mode of resistance as being a subtle snare ; as bad, at least, as that of the " German Christians." I know quite well what I am doing. God can bear me witness that I would not like to quieten anybody who is now disturbed. But I would like to put this question to any of those who are in this way disturbed : Are they really, seriously disturbed ? *So* disturbed that they cannot allow themselves to be quietened any longer by any disturbing Church-politics ? *So* disturbed?—that in the end the only thing left to them is *to be* the Church—which word they take so often on their lips, of course, quite sincerely, yet it is probable often without meaning— the Church which is the Fellowship of the Called, the Hearers, the Obedient, the Awakened, the Pray-ers, the Hopers and Hasteners. *So* disturbed ? —that for these to break away from *being* such a Church is banned and barred. So that for them there is nothing else for it but, at the one sacred place appointed to them, to fight this fight out— the fight, the seriousness of which even now they obliterate with their battle-cry, in the conflict into which no one else ever sent them but their own disturbed and despairing hearts !

Theological existence, in the situation created once more by the " German Christians " to-day, even more than yesterday, would simply mean " That we henceforth be no more children tossed to and fro and carried about by every wind of doctrine " (*Eph.* iv. 14). May God have mercy on us for the lack of steadfastness that has been manifest everywhere, because of the dominion of " the Prince of the Power of the air " (*Eph.* ii. 2 ; German version). There should have been no need for it, and, blessed be God ! there is no necessity that it should be so again to-morrow.

" THE ONE THING NEEDFUL "

I come back to where I set out. All that has been said as to " the situation " has no separate significance for what I meant to say. I have not " broken silence," because I fancied that any remarks of mine on the bishop controversy, the " German Christians," and so on, were indispensable.

But I did desire, indeed, I felt I had to say this much, with reference to some of the problems which are disturbing us all to-day. This single thing I have to say to the evangelical theologians : " We have to preserve our life as theologians to-day ; to-day—more than yesterday. We have to run the plain, straightforward course set before us, untrammelled and unfalteringly, and ' if sinners entice thee, consent thou not ' (*Prov.* i. 10)."

If someone should now reply and say : " In view of the great movement now sweeping through the nation, in view of the great task up to which it must now live, it is all too small, all too narrow, indeed too self-centred to say that we have to preserve our existence as theologians at all costs." To this I would reply : " Friend, let us think both *spiritually* and, consequently, *realistically*. Theological existence is certainly not an end in itself, as certainly God Himself was not content to be an end in Himself, Who rather ' spared not His only Son but delivered Him up for us all : how shall He not with Him freely give us all things ? ' (*Rom.* viii. 32)."

If God in Christ is utterly for us men, then the Church too, as being "the place where His glory dwelleth," must be utterly for man, and therefore for the German people, and therefore be the German Evangelical Church for the German Evangelical people, and we theologians of Germany must also be really and sincerely for this people. But we are under obligation to be what *we* are, and true to the mission entrusted to *us* : to serve the Word of God within this nation. If we pursue other ideals and aims, which have *not* been committed to us, we sin, not only against God, but also against the people.

But it lies in the very nature of this commission, that it cannot possibly be subordinated to, or co-ordinated with, any other interests that may move us. Again, we sin, not only against God but against the people, if this order of preference of our pursuits be allowed in the least to be shaken. And this commission will be carried through : it is much the same whether the people want it or not. We need not expect any gratitude or glory ; nor need we be surprised if from all sides we earn the very opposite through carrying on. Eventually, we have to accept having to be alone, simply for the sake of the people's fellowship. We should be sinning not only against God, but also against the people, if we were to go *with* the people, instead of standing *for* them.

The Nation, even and precisely the German Nation of the year 1933, cannot do without this carrying out of the mission that has been entrusted to us theologians. To-day there has been appointed to it something quite extraordinary in its prospects— that the people should be united and free on one way which its leaders have made plain to its understanding, and which the people have elected to travel with those leaders. But the Nation will need the admonition and the comfort of the Word of God, even when it shall have reached its goal, all the more to-day when it is standing at the beginning of the road. And this all the more as, for the sake of those promises, much had to be taken away to-day which the people earlier could enjoy, and which indeed, all too foolishly and without sense of responsibility, they have been glad of. All that was called Liberty, Justice, Spirit only a year ago and for a hundred years farther back, where has it all gone ? Now, these are all temporal, material, earthly goods ! " All flesh is as grass . . ." No doubt !

There is no doubt that many people in olden times, and later, have had to do without these proffered goods, and have been able to, if the bold enterprise of the " Totalitarian State " demands it of them. " But the Word of our God abideth for ever," and, consequently, it is true and indispensable every day ; for every day hastens into Eternity. Because of this, theology and the Church cannot enter upon a winter sleep within the " Total State " ; no moratorium and no "assimilation " (*Gleichschaltung*) can befall them. They are the natural frontiers of everything, even of the " Totalitarian State." For even in this " Total State " the nation always lives by the Word of God, the content of which is " forgiveness of sins, resurrection of the body, and life everlasting." To this Word the Church and theology have to render service for the people. Because of this, Church and Theology are the frontiers, the bounds, of the State. They are this for the salvation of the people : *that* salvation which neither the State nor yet the Church can create, but which the Church is called upon to proclaim. The Church *must* be allowed to be true to her proper pragmatic function, and be *willing* to be true. In the particular concern entrusted to us, we theologians must be awake, " as a sparrow on the house-tops " (*Psalm* cii. 7) ; on the earth also, but under the open, wide, but infinite open heavens. If it so be that the German Evangelical theologian should still remain awake, on the watch, or if he have gone to sleep, to-day, to-day once more, Oh ! that once more he were awake !

(*Finished, Sunday, June 25th,* 1933.)